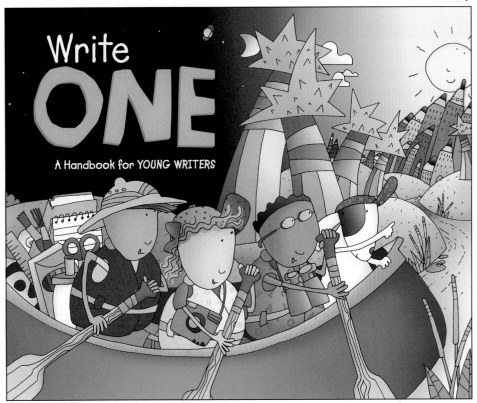

**Write ONE**

A Handbook for YOUNG WRITERS

Authors **Dave Kemper, Carol Elsholz, Patrick Sebranek**
Illustrator **Chris Krenzke**

# WRITE SOURCE®

GREAT SOURCE EDUCATION GROUP
a Houghton Mifflin Company
Wilmington, Massachusetts

# Acknowledgements

We're grateful to many people who helped bring *Write One* to life. First, we must thank all the students from across the country who contributed their writing models and ideas. Also, thanks to the writers, editors, and teachers who helped make this book a reality.

Betsey Bystol

Nancy Koceja

Dian Lynch

Jim MacCall

Deb Pingle

Pat Reigel

In addition, we want to thank our Write Source/Great Source team for all their help: Laura Bachman, Colleen Belmont, Sherry Gordon, Lois Krenzke, Ellen Leitheusser, Sue Paro, and Sandy Wagner.

Trademarks and trade names are shown in this book strictly for illustrative purposes and are the property of their respective owners. The authors' references herein should not be regarded as affecting their validity.

Printed in the United States of America

International Standard Book Number: 0-669-49011-3 (hardcover)

1 2 3 4 5 6 7 8 9     -RRDW-     06 05 04 03 02

International Standard Book Number: 0-669-49012-1 (softcover)

1 2 3 4 5 6 7 8 9     -RRDW-     06 05 04 03 02

# Write One You'll Have Fun!

**The Process of Writing** This part tells you all about being a writer.

**The Forms of Writing** Here you'll learn about writing notes, stories, poems, and more.

**Tools of Learning** In this part you'll learn about listening, speaking, and reading and writing new words.

**Proofreader's Guide** In this part you'll find out how to use capital letters and punctuation.

**Student Almanac** This part has maps, math charts, pictures, names of animals and places, and lots more.

# Table of Contents

## The **Process** of Writing

### All About Writing

**12** Jenny Writes

**22** Traits of Good Writing

**24** Steps in the Writing Process

   **24** Plan

   **25** Write

   **26** Revise

   **26** Check

   **27** Publish

# The Forms of Writing

## Personal Writing

30 Writing in Journals
32 Writing Lists
34 Writing Friendly Notes
36 Writing E-Mail Messages
38 Writing Friendly Letters
40 Writing Stories About Me

## Subject Writing

44 Writing About Others
46 Writing a Description
48 How-To Writing
50 Writing Captions
52 Making Alphabet Books
54 Writing About Books

## Research Writing

58 Writing Reports
62 Writing in Learning Logs

## Story and Poetry Writing

66 Writing Stories
68 Writing Poems
72 Writing with Patterns

The **Process** of Writing

The **Forms** of Writing

The **Tools** of Learning

**Proofreader's** Guide

Student **Almanac**

# The **Tools** of Learning

## Listening and Speaking Skills

**76** Listening to Others

**78** Speaking to Others

**80** Working Together

## Reading and Word-Study Skills

**84** Reading to Understand

**86** Reading New Words

    **88** Consonant Blends

    **89** Consonant Digraphs

    **90** Long Vowels

    **91** Short Vowels

    **92** Rhyming Families

    **94** Contractions

    **95** Compound Words

**96** Using Alphabet Lists

# Proofreader's Guide

## Rules for Writing

**126** Writing Sentences

**128** Using Capital Letters

**129** Making Plurals

**130** Using Punctuation

**134** Understanding Our Language

**136** Using Everyday Words

**140** Using the Right Word

The **Process** of Writing

The **Forms** of Writing

The **Tools** of Learning

**Proofreader's** Guide

Student **Almanac**

B A
C
D E
F
G H
I
J
K L
M
N
O P
Q R
S
T U
V
W
X

# Student **Almanac**

## Lists, Maps, and Theme Words

**148** Practicing Handwriting

    **150** Manuscript Models

    **152** Continuous Stroke Models

**154** Using a Computer

**156** Using Maps

    **157** World Map

    **158** North America Map

    **159** United States Map

**160** Working with Math

    **161** Telling Time

    **162** Numbers 1 to 100

    **163** Place Value

    **164** Bar Graphs

    **165** Money

    **166** Addition and Subtraction

    **167** Fractions

**168** Using Theme Words

**169** Days of the Week

**170** Months of the Year

**172** Seasons and Weather

**174** Numbers and Colors

**176** Places

**178** Parks

**180** Plants

**182** Food Pyramid

**184** Animals of the . . .

**186** Five Senses

**188** Index

# The **Process** of Writing

# All About Writing

In this part of your handbook, you will meet Jenny, Luke, Rosa, and Ben. They are writers. You can be a writer, too.

# Jenny Writes

It's writing time in Room 101. Luke is planning a story. Rosa is writing a poem. Ben is writing something silly.

Jenny wonders, "What can I write?"

Jenny asks Luke what he's writing. Luke tells her he's writing a dog story. It's about his three dogs. Luke knows a lot about dogs.

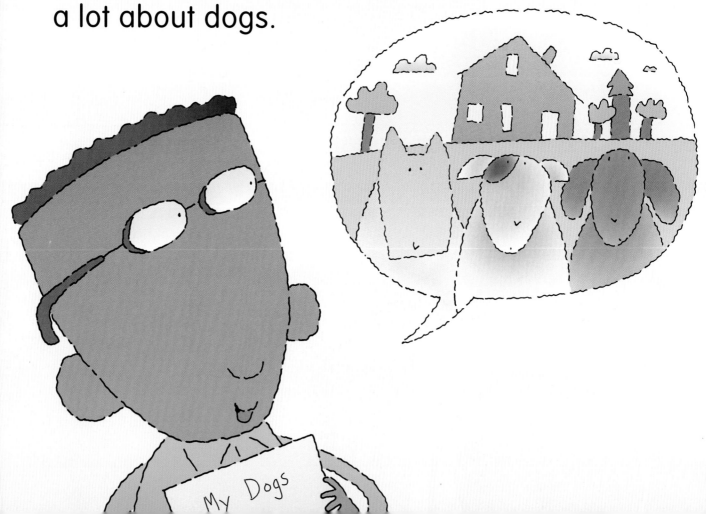

Jenny still wonders, "What can I write?"

Jenny asks Rosa about her poem.
Rosa reads it to Jenny. It's about
the time she went fishing with her
grandpa. Rosa's poem rhymes.

How we wish
we had a fish.

fish

Jenny still wonders, "What can I write?"

Then Ben pops up next to Jenny's desk. Ben shows her the silly note he wrote. Jenny and Ben laugh at the note.

Suddenly Jenny thinks, "This note gives me an idea."

ABCDEFGHIJKLMNOPQRSTUVWXYZ

Just like her friends, Jenny begins to write and draw.

Jenny writes a note to her mom and dad.

Hi Mom and Dad,
I like cats.
Luke has three
BIG DOGS!
I wish we had
one little cat.

Love,
Jenny

# Traits of Good Writing

Good writing has these special things:

## Interesting Ideas

Write about things that interest you.

## Clear Order

Plan a beginning, a middle, and an ending.

## Well-Chosen Words

Find the right words to say what you mean.

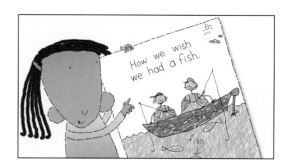

## Personal Voice

Make your writing sound like you.

## Smooth Sentences

Write sentences that are easy to read out loud.

## Correct Copy

Find ways to spell words. Get help with your punctuation, too.

# Steps in the Writing Process

The **writing process** has five steps: plan, write, revise, check, and publish.

**1**

**PLAN**

- Talk.
- Draw.
- Think.
- Write lists.

Things Pets Need

1. food
2. water
3. love
4. a plas to sleep
5. toys

## 2

## WRITE

- Write sentences about the topic.
- Spell words the best you can.
- Use your plan as you write.

SPOT

Things Pets Need

Pets need food and water. Pets like to be loved. they need a plas to sleep. Pets like to have toys.

## 3

### REVISE

- Read it aloud.
- Does it sound right?
- Make changes.

## 4

### CHECK

- Capitals
- Punctuation
- Spelling

Things Pets Need

Pets need food and ∧ fresh

water. Pets like to be

loved. They need a place ~~plas~~

to sleep. Pets like to have

fun toys.

**5**

## PUBLISH

- Make a neat copy.
- Share it with others.
- Put it in a class book.

### Things Pets Need

Pets need food and fresh water. Pets like to be loved. They need a place to sleep. Pets like to have fun.

by Krista

A
B
C
D
E
F
G
H
I
J
K
L
M
N
O
P
Q
R
S
T
U
V
W
X
Y
Z

# The **Forms** of Writing

# Personal Writing

Your life is full of ideas you can share. Write about these ideas in stories, letters, and journals.

# Writing in Journals

A **journal** is your very own place for writing. You can write in your journal every day.

- Write the date.

- Draw a picture if you want to.

- Write about things you do and think about.

October 7

I ride my bike fast.
I can make it jump.
My bike is red.

A journal is waiting for your words.

**Ideas for your journal:**

▸ A story about a friend

▸ A wish list

▸ Something you like to do

▸ Places you like to go

▸ Poems

▸ Questions you want to ask

▸ A list of books you've read

▸ Jokes

# Writing Lists

**Lists** are easy to write. They can be long or short, serious or silly. You can write lists for many reasons.

**Show what you know.**

Wild Animals
lion
deer
snake
wolf
ape
hippo

Have fun.

Remember things.

Happy Words

joy
sun
smile
jump

Store

corn
milk
apples
peanut butter

**More list ideas:**
- Favorite things
- Pets
- Games
- Words
- Friends
- Things to do
- Colors

# Writing Friendly Notes

Writing a **friendly note** is fun. Your note can be an invitation, a reply, or a thank-you.

## An Invitation

Lea,
You are funny.
Do you want to
play at my house?
Say YES.
Michelle

## A Reply

Dear Michelle,
I can come
to your house.
Tell your mom
to call my mom.
Lea

## A Thank-You Note

Hi Michelle,
I had fun at your house. Thanks for the ladybug pin.

Lea

### Other note ideas:

- ▶ Facts about things
- ▶ Kind things
- ▶ Funny things

# Writing E-Mail Messages

You can write an **e-mail message** without using paper or pencil. You write it on a computer, using a keyboard.

There are four important parts to e-mail:

**1 From:**
(Your address will appear here.)

**2 To:**
(Type the address you are sending to.)

**3 Subject:**
(Type what your message is about.)

**4 Message:**
(Type your message here.)

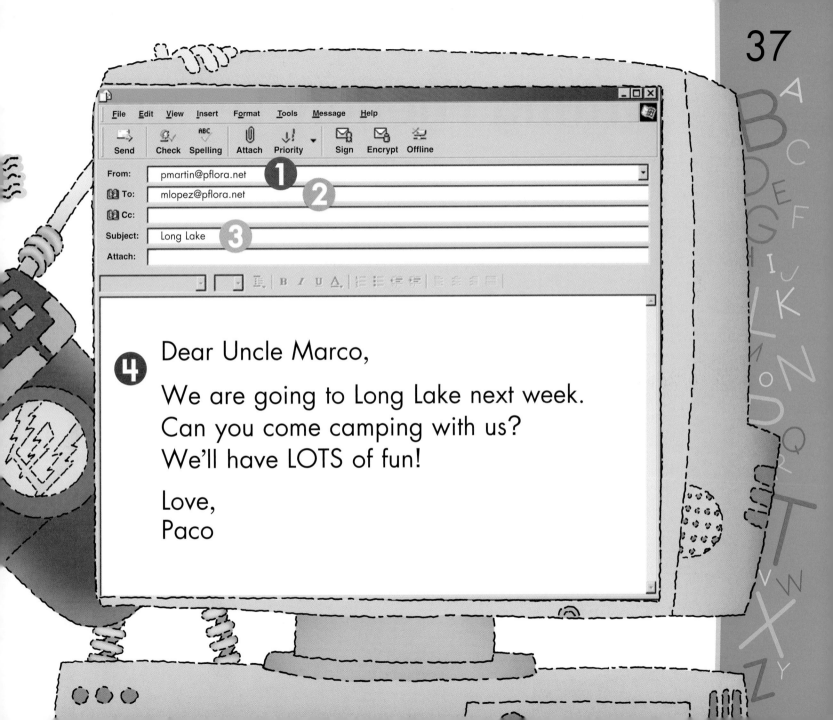

**File** **Edit** **View** **Insert** **Format** **Tools** **Message** **Help**

Send | Check | Spelling | Attach | Priority | Sign | Encrypt | Offline

From: pmartin@pflora.net **1** **2**
To: mlopez@pflora.net
Cc:
Subject: Long Lake **3**
Attach:

**4**

Dear Uncle Marco,

We are going to Long Lake next week.
Can you come camping with us?
We'll have LOTS of fun!

Love,
Paco

# Writing Friendly Letters

You can write a **friendly letter** to someone near or faraway.

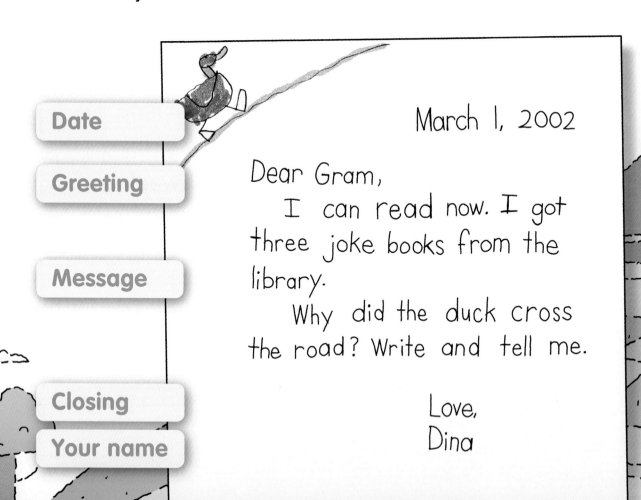

**Date**

March 1, 2002

**Greeting**

Dear Gram,
   I can read now. I got three joke books from the library.
   Why did the duck cross the road? Write and tell me.

**Message**

**Closing**

Love,
Dina

**Your name**

# Sending Your Letter

Address the envelope. Add a stamp.
Then send your letter.

**Your address**

DINA BENJAMIN
440 OAK ST
DENVER CO 80202

MRS JUDITH MURPHY
86 PARK AVE
RICHMOND VA 23201

**Mailing address**

# Writing Stories About Me

A **story about me** is about a special time in your life. A cluster can help you plan your story.

**Make a cluster.**

Jesse

Josh came home.

I held him.

A Happy Day

He didn't cry.

He was in a yellow blanket.

**Write a story from the cluster.**

A Happy Day

One day baby Josh came home. He was in a yellow blanket. My mom let me hold him. He was blowing bubbles. He didn't cry.

by Jesse

# Subject Writing

It's fun to talk about interesting people, places, and things. You can write about them, too.

B A
C
D
E
F
G H
I
J
K L
M
N
O
P
Q
R
S
T
U
V
W
X
Y
Z

# Writing About Others

Do you know someone you can write about?
Start with an important idea about this person.
Then write details that tell about your idea.

**Important idea**

**Details**

**Silly Nick**

**My cousin Nick is silly. He puts potato chips in his soup. He wears two different socks. Sometimes he wears a bow tie. When he sleeps over at my house, he brings his goldfish along.**

**by Timothy**

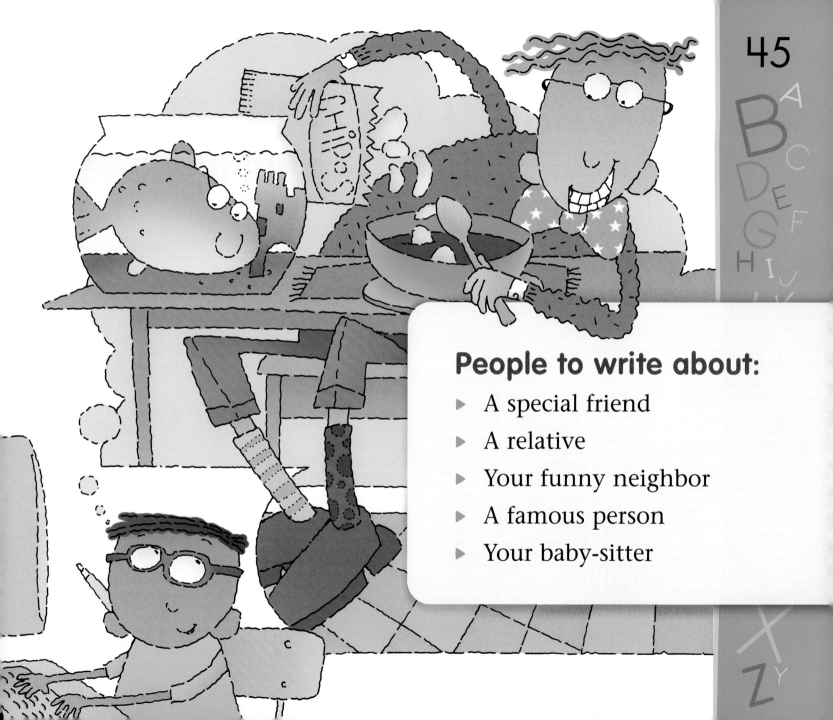

## People to write about:

- A special friend
- A relative
- Your funny neighbor
- A famous person
- Your baby-sitter

# Writing a Description

You can write **descriptions** about people, places, or things.

- Tell how something **LOOKS**.
- Tell how something **FEELS**.

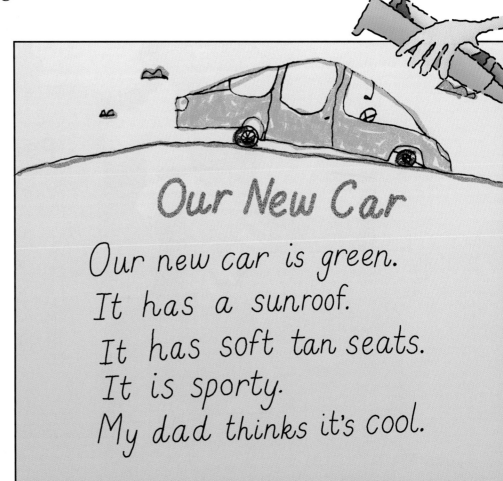

## Our New Car

Our new car is green.
It has a sunroof.
It has soft tan seats.
It is sporty.
My dad thinks it's cool.

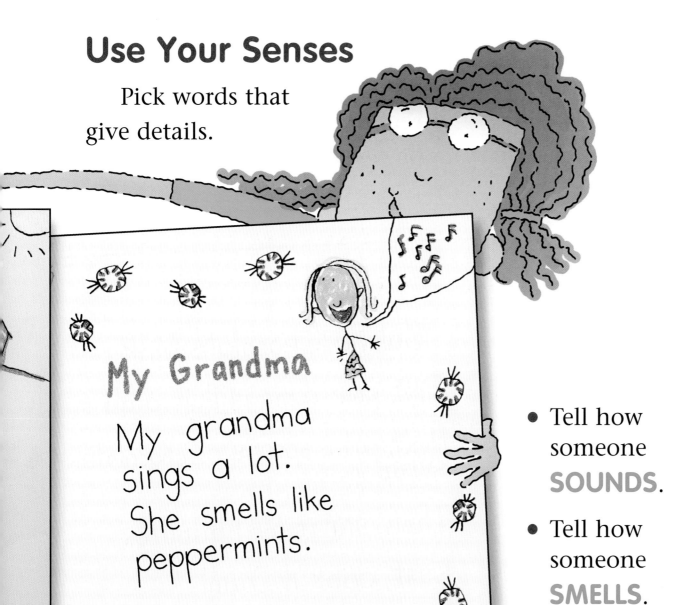

## Use Your Senses

Pick words that give details.

**My Grandma**

My grandma sings a lot. She smells like peppermints.

- Tell how someone **SOUNDS**.

- Tell how someone **SMELLS**.

# How-To Writing

When you write **directions**, you tell how to do something. Use *words* or *numbers* to put the steps in order.

**Start with words.**

Making Chocolate Milk

First, pour some milk in a glass.

Next, put 2 spoons of chocolate syrup in.

Then, stir it for 1 minute.

Last, drink it. Yum!

by Michael

**Start with numbers.**

Getting Ready for School
by Bet

1. Wash up and get dresse
2. Eat breakfast.
3. Brush your teeth.
4. Grab your schoolbag

**Other dire**

▸ Taking c
▸ Making
▸ Makin

# Writing Captions

Adding **captions** to pictures makes them more interesting. Captions give you special information.

Journals go everywhere!

We love reading time.

MIGRATION

Butterflies move from place to place.

# Making Alphabet Books

Making an **alphabet book** is as easy as ABC. You can make one by yourself or with your class.

**1** Choose a topic.

**2** List words about the topic.

## Words About Our School

| | | | |
|---|---|---|---|
| A | art | G | gym |
| B | bus | H | heart |
| C | calendar | I | ice cream |
| D | dancing | J | jokes |
| E | Eastview | K | kindness |
| F | friends | L | lunch |

H

**H** is for heart.
Your heart keeps you
alive. There are
good hearts in
this school.
♥     by Adam

F

G

We ha
on Tue
and it
gym f

M

def
rstuvw
fghijklmn
xyzabcde
pqrstuvwx
ghijklmnopq

3 Make a
page for
each letter.

4 Put the pages
together
in a book.

ABC'S
of
Eastview
School

A
B
C
D
E
F
G
H
I
J
K
L
M
N
O
P
Q
R
S
T
U
V
W
X
Y
Z

# Writing About Books

Reading books is fun. Writing about books is fun, too. You can write a poem, make a poster, or tell about books in other ways.

**Write a poem.**

Book <u>Three Ducks Went Wandering</u>

by <u>Ron Roy</u>

One sunny day
the ducks ran away.
They wanted to play.

**Make a poster.**

READ
Sheep Out to Eat
by Nancy Shaw

It's very funny.
The sheep like green
food the best.

## Telling About Books

### Do a retelling.

- Tell important parts and favorite parts.

### Do a dramatic reading.

- Read favorite parts and funny parts.

# Research Writing

When you do research, you find new ideas and amazing facts. It's exciting to write and share these ideas with others.

# Writing Reports

When you learn a lot about a subject, you can write about it in a **report**.

**1**

## PLAN

- Learn about your topic.
- List or cluster the important facts.

## 2

## WRITE

- Use your list or cluster to help you write.
- Write sentences about the topic.
- Spell words the best you can.

Spiders have eight legs. Spiders have fangs. Some spiders are poisonous. Spiders spin webs. Some spiders live undrgrowd. Did you know that spiders aren't insects.

## 3

### REVISE

- Read it aloud.
- Does it sound right?
- Make changes.

## 4

### CHECK

- Capitals
- Punctuation
- Spelling

Spiders have eight legs.

Spiders have ^two fangs. Some

spiders are poisonous.

^Most Spiders spin webs. Some

spiders live ~~undrgrowd.~~ underground

Did you know that

spiders aren't insects~~.~~?

## 5

## PUBLISH

- Make a neat copy.
- Share it with others.
- Put it in a class book.

April 21

Spiders

    Spiders have eight legs. Spiders have two fangs. Some spiders are poisonous. Most spiders spin webs. Some spiders live underground. Did you know that spiders aren't insects?

by Todd

# Writing in Learning Logs

You can write about your school work in a **learning log**. You can write facts, ask questions, and list new words.

## Science Learning Log

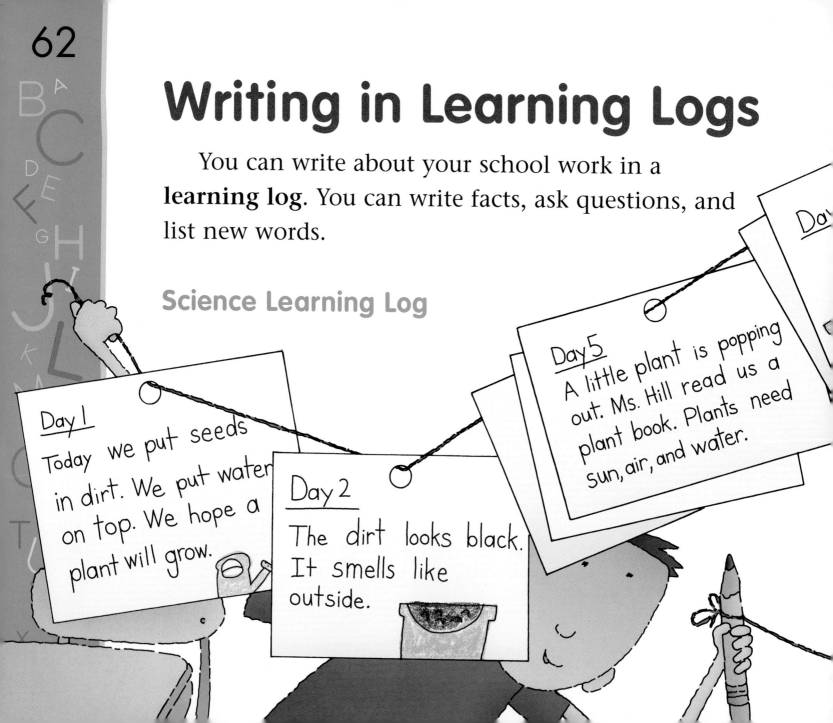

Day 1
Today we put seeds in dirt. We put water on top. We hope a plant will grow.

Day 2
The dirt looks black. It smells like outside.

Day 5
A little plant is popping out. Ms. Hill read us a plant book. Plants need sun, air, and water.

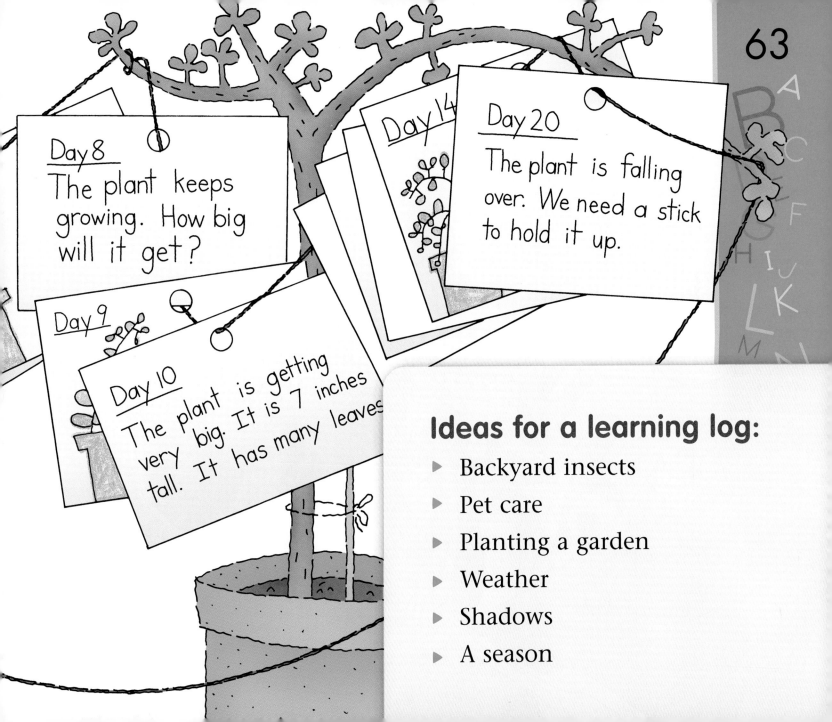

**Day 8**
The plant keeps growing. How big will it get?

**Day 9**

**Day 10**
The plant is getting very big. It is 7 inches tall. It has many leaves

**Day 14**

**Day 20**
The plant is falling over. We need a stick to hold it up.

## Ideas for a learning log:

▸ Backyard insects

▸ Pet care

▸ Planting a garden

▸ Weather

▸ Shadows

▸ A season

# Story and Poetry Writing

Do you like to listen to stories and poems? This section will help you write stories and poems of your own. Have fun!

# Writing Stories

With a little planning, writing a made-up story is easy—and a lot of fun!

You can **plan** a story with words.

- Name the characters.

- Tell what happens.

You can **plan** a story with pictures.

- Show what happens with pictures you draw or collect.

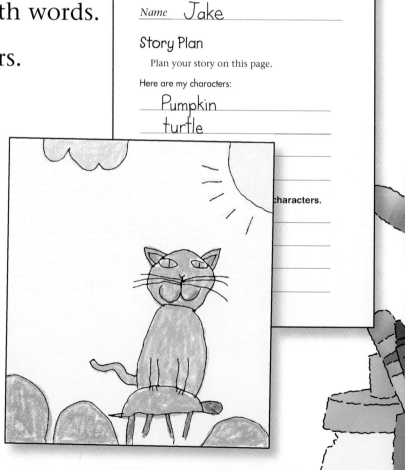

Name  Jake

Story Plan

Plan your story on this page.

Here are my characters:

Pumpkin

turtle

characters.

After Jake planned his story, he wrote it down. His story has good order.

**Pumpkin the Cat**

**by Jake**

**Beginning**

**Middle**

**Ending**

One sunny day Pumpkin the cat sat on a rock. The rock moved! It was a turtle! Pumpkin got so scared, she ran away. She didn't come back until late at night. She never sat on a green rock again.

# Writing Poems

**Writing poems** is like making little word pictures. Think of the best words to use in your poems.

## Couplet

- Write **two** lines that rhyme.

> Sometimes comets in space
> Look like they're having a race.
> – Max

## Triplet

- Write **three** lines that rhyme.

> Colors, colors everywhere,
> Colors here and colors there,
> Colors on the shirt I wear.
> – Shiere

## Quatrain

- Write **four** lines.
  Make at least two lines rhyme.

Polka dots, polka dots
On my dress.
How many polka dots?
Can you guess?

      – Kathleen

The owl in the tree was talking to me.
I heard him say, "Good night."
My sister says that owls don't talk.
But I know she's not right.

      – Shavonn

# More Poem Ideas

## Tongue Twister

- Begin most of the words with the **same sound**.

> Jackson jumped and jiggled, just like a jumping jack.

## Cinquain

- Write **five** lines. Use the form below.

One word (the topic)
Two words
Three words
Four words
One word

> Shadow
> Tall, short,
> Hops, waves, jumps.
> Follows where I go.
> Me!

## List Poem

- Make a **list**. Here are three list poems.

Joker
On the bus
Silly
Eats cold pizza.

A name and describing words

Ideas

Snow is everywhere.
  Snow is on our school.
  Snow is on the swings.
  Snow is on the trees.
  Snow is on the houses.
  Snow is under our feet.
  Snow is on our noses.
Snow is everywhere!

  – Clarendon School
    Room 36

ABC's

Aunt
Bonnie
Can
Dance
Every
Friday

A B C D E F G H I J K L M N O P Q R S T U V W X Y Z

# Writing with Patterns

Many songs, poems, and stories follow a pattern.
Most patterns have rhyming words and a special beat.

## Pattern in a Song

Once you learn the pattern, write your own words.

### The Itsy Bitsy Spider

The itsy bitsy spider
went up the **waterspout**.
Down came the rain
and washed the spider **out**.

Out came the sun
and dried up all the rain.
Then the itsy bitsy spider
went up the spout again.

## Pattern in a NEW Song

### The Friendly, Funny Lobster

The friendly, funny lobster
climbed out of the blue sea.
He crawled across the sand
and sat down next to me.

He reached out a claw
and then shook hands with me.
Then the friendly, funny lobster
crept back into the sea.

**More patterns:**

- The Gingerbread Man
- Over in the Meadow
- This Old Man
- Miss Mary Mack

# The **Tools** of Learning

# Listening and Speaking Skills

This section gives you tips about being a good reader. Being a good reader can help you be a good writer, too.

# Listening to Others

You can listen to your parents and your friends. You can listen to reporters on television and teachers in school. Listening is fun. It is also a great way to learn new things.

# Being a Good Listener

- **BE QUIET.**

- **LOOK** at the person who is speaking.

- **LISTEN** for important words.

- **ASK** questions after the person stops talking.

# Speaking to Others

Do you have something special to share?
Did you get a new toy, read a good book, or find
an interesting rock? You can show it to your
classmates. You can tell them about it, too.

## Show-and-Share Tips

- **SHOW** what you are going to talk about.

- **LOOK** at your classmates.

- **SPEAK** loudly and slowly.

- **MAKE SURE** everyone can see what you are showing.

- **SHARE** important details.

- **END** with one last interesting idea.

# Working Together

It's fun to do things together. You can play games, be on a team, or work in a group. Everyone in the group needs to be polite and take turns. When you work together, you can get things done. You can have fun, too.

# Teamwork Tips

- **TAKE TURNS**—one person talks at a time.
- **LOOK** at the person who is speaking.
- **LISTEN** to what others have to say.
- **SHARE** your ideas, too.
- **USE** polite words as you work together.

# Reading and Word-Study Skills

Knowing letter names and sounds helps you with your reading. It helps you with your spelling, too.

# Reading to Understand

Reading takes lots of thinking. You should think before, during, and after reading.

## Think **Before** Reading

**LOOK** over your reading.

- Check the title.
- Look at the pictures.

**PREDICT** what will be in the reading.

## Think **During** Reading

**TRY** to picture what you are reading about.

**CHECK** to see if your predictions are right or wrong.

## Think **After** Reading

**TELL** yourself or someone else what the reading was about.

**ASK** for help if you didn't understand part of the reading.

# Reading New Words

There are many ways to read new words.

Try these tips for reading new words.

**LISTEN** for sounds.

- Say the word slowly and listen for sounds at the beginning, middle, and end.

**LOOK** for parts or patterns you know.

- If you can read but, you can read
  butter and button.

- If you can read hill, you can read will.

- If you can read play, you can read playing.

**LOOK** and **THINK**.

- Read the whole sentence.

- Ask yourself what word would make sense
  in the sentence.

- Look at the pictures on the page.

**ASK** for help.

# Consonant Blends

**Consonant blends** are two or more consonants that come together and keep their own sounds.

| | |
|---|---|
| fr • pr • dr | **fr**iends **pr**etty **dr**ess |
| bl • cl • fl | **bl**ue **cl**oud **fl**ag |
| sp • st • sn | **sp**ot **st**ep **sn**ow |

**Blends at the end of words:**

de**sk**    be**st**    pi**nk**

# Consonant Digraphs

**Consonant digraphs** are two consonants that come together and make one sound.

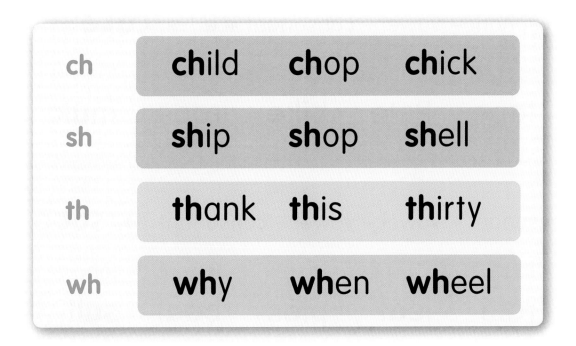

| | | | |
|---|---|---|---|
| ch | **ch**ild | **ch**op | **ch**ick |
| sh | **sh**ip | **sh**op | **sh**ell |
| th | **th**ank | **th**is | **th**irty |
| wh | **wh**y | **wh**en | **wh**eel |

**Digraphs at the end of words:**

cat**ch**    wi**sh**    ma**th**

# Long Vowels

Here are two patterns for long vowel words:

consonant – vowel – consonant + e → cāke

| long a | long e | long i | long o | long u |
|--------|--------|--------|--------|--------|
| tape | Pete | bike | rope | mule |

consonant – vowel – vowel – consonant → sōap

| long a | long e | long i | long o | long u |
|--------|--------|--------|--------|--------|
| rain | leaf | pies | boat | suit |

# Short Vowels

Most short vowel words have this pattern:

consonant – **v**owel – **c**onsonant  →  **s**ŭ**n**

| short a | short e | short i | short o | short u |
|---------|---------|---------|---------|---------|
| m**a**p | b**e**ll | p**i**n | h**o**p | b**u**g |

5    6    7    8    9    10    11    12

# Rhyming Families

Rhyming helps you read and write new words.

**If you know these words,** you can read and write these.

| hat | **bat** **sat** **flat** |
|-----|--------------------------|

| fun | **run** **bun** **sun** |
|-----|-------------------------|

| mop | **top** **hop** **crop** |
|-----|--------------------------|

If you know these words, you can read and write these.

| | | | |
|---|---|---|---|
| fish | **wish** | **dish** | **swish** |
| cake | **lake** | **bake** | **snake** |
| like | **bike** | **hike** | **Mike** |
| rain | **pain** | **train** | **grain** |

# Contractions

A **contraction** is one shorter word made from two words. You leave some letters out.

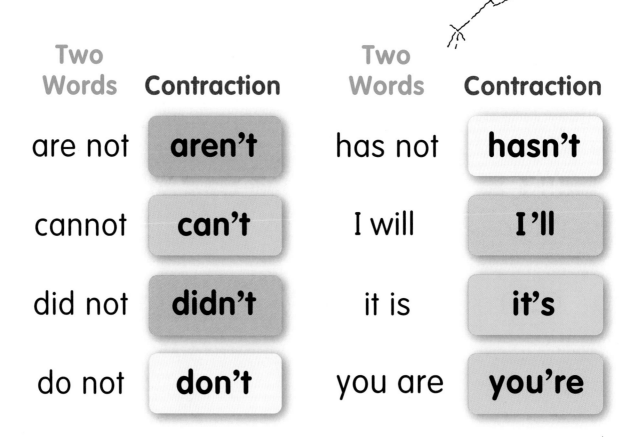

| Two Words | Contraction | Two Words | Contraction |
|-----------|-------------|-----------|-------------|
| are not | **aren't** | has not | **hasn't** |
| cannot | **can't** | I will | **I'll** |
| did not | **didn't** | it is | **it's** |
| do not | **don't** | you are | **you're** |

# Compound Words

A **compound word** is a longer word made from two shorter words.

| Two Words | | Compound Word |
|---|---|---|
| base + ball | = | **baseball** |
| fish + hook | = | **fishhook** |
| pop + corn | = | **popcorn** |
| snow + flake | = | **snowflake** |
| space + ship | = | **spaceship** |

# Using Alphabet Lists

The alphabet can give you ideas for writing list poems and lists of words.

**Alphabet List Poem**

Alligator **sits,**
Butterfly **flits.**

Cup **of tea,**
Ducks **at sea.**

Eggs **to cook,**
Fish **in a brook.**

Girl named Mary,
Hat for Harry.

Igloo white,
Jacket bright.

Kite in the sky,
Ladybug shy.

Mouse near a hole,
Nest like a bowl.

Octopus below,
Penguin in the snow.

Quilt for a bed,
Rocket that's red.

Socks for running,
Turtle goes sunning.

Umbrella for showers,
Vase full of flowers.

Wagon to pull,
Box full of wool.

Yarn soft and blue,
Zipper-dee-do!

# Aa

**alligator**

bat
map
Sam

**ape**

cake
play
rain

# Bb

**butterfly**

baby

balloon

bird

book

bow

boy

bug

A
B
C
D
E
F
G
H
I
J
K
L
M
N
O
P
Q
R
S
T
U
V
W
X
Y
Z

B C D E F G H I J K L M N O P Q R S T U V W X Y Z A

# Cc

**cup**

candle

cat

coat

**cereal**

cent

circle

city

# Dd

## ducks

daddy
daisy
day
dinner
dinosaur
dog
door

A B C D E F G H I J K L M N O P Q R S T U V W X Y Z

B A
C
D
F E
G
H I
J
K L
M
N O
P
Q
S R
T
U
W V
X
Y Z

# E e

**eggs**

deck
Meg
pen

**eagle**

bean
Pete
see

# Ff

**fish**

family
father
feet
finger
fire
food
fun

A
B
C
D
E
F
G
H
I
J
K
L
M
N
O
P
Q
R
S
T
U
V
W
X
Y
Z

B
A
C
D
E
F
G
H
I
J
K
L
M
N
O
P
Q
R
S
T
U
V
W
X
Y
Z

# Gg

**girl**

gate
goat
gold

**gem**

gerbil
giant
giraffe

# Hh

**hat**

hair
hand
head
home
horse
house
hug

# I i

**igloo**

bib
hill
pig

**ice skate**

bike
pie
white

# Jj

**jacket**

jar

jelly

jet

job

joy

juice

jungle

A B C D E F G H I J K L M N O P Q R S T U V W X Y Z

B A C D E F G H I J K L M N O P Q R S T U V W X Y Z

# Kk

**kite**

kangaroo
key
kid
king
kiss
kitchen
kitten

# Ll

**ladybug**

land
laugh
leaf
leg
letter
light
love

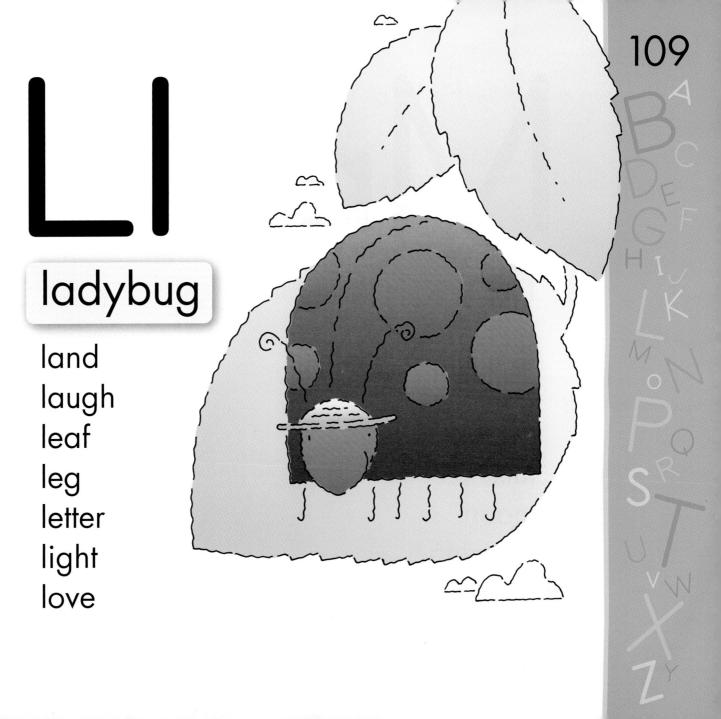

B
A
C
D
E
F
G
H
I
J
K
L
M
N
O
P
Q
R
S
T
U
V
W
X
Y
Z

# Mm

## mouse

mammal

man

mask

milk

moon

morning

mother

# Nn

**nest**

name

necklace

neighbor

nickel

night

nose

nurse

A
B
C
D
E
F
G
H
I
J
K
L
M
N
O
P
Q
R
S
T
U
V
W
X
Y
Z

B A
C
D
E
F
G H
I
J
K L
M N
O P
Q
R S
T U
V
W
X Y
Z

# Oo

## octopus

box
dog
rock

## oak tree

bone
goat
no

# P p

**penguin**

paper
party
pencil
people
pet
picture
popcorn

A
B
C
D
E
F
G
H
I
J
K
L
M
N
O
P
Q
R
S
T
U
V
W
X
Y
Z

# Qq

**quilt**

quart
quarter
queen
question
question mark
quiet
quiz

# Rr

**rocket**

rabbit
rain
rat
ring
road
room
rose

A
B
C
D
E
F
G
H
I
J
K
L
M
N
O
P
Q
R
S
T
U
V
W
X
Y
Z

# S s

socks

sailboat

sand

seed

sister

soap

song

sun

# T t

**turtle**

table
teacher
television
today
tooth
toy
turkey

A B C D E F G H I J K L M N O P Q R S T U V W X Y Z

# Uu

**umbrella**

duck
fun
rug

**unicycle**

mule
Sue
suit

# Vv

## vase

valentine
vegetable
vest
vine
violin
visit
voice

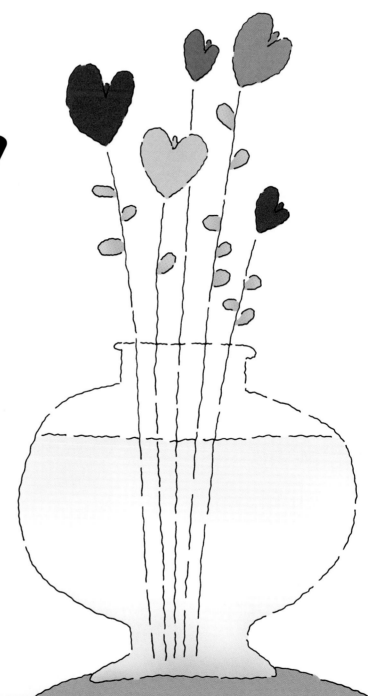

A B C D E F G H I J K L M N O P Q R S T U V W X Y Z

B A
C
D
E
F G
H I
J
K L
M N
O P
Q
S R
T U
V
W
X Y
Z

# Ww

**wagon**

water

wind

window

wing

wish

wood

worm

# X x

**bo<u>x</u>**

ax
fix
fox
Max
ox
six
wax

A B C D E F G H I J K L M N O P Q R S T U V W X Y Z

# Y y

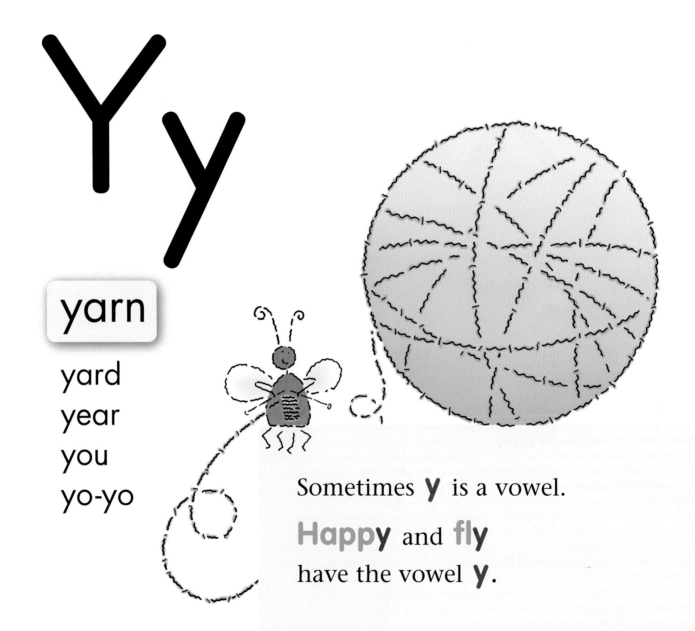

**yarn**

yard

year

you

yo-yo

Sometimes **y** is a vowel.

**Happy** and **fly**

have the vowel **y**.

# Zz

## zipper

zebra

zero

zigzag

zone

zoo

zucchini

# Proofreader's
## Guide

# Rules for Writing

All writers follow rules. In this section, you can find lots of rules to help you with your writing.

# Writing Sentences

A **sentence** states a complete thought.

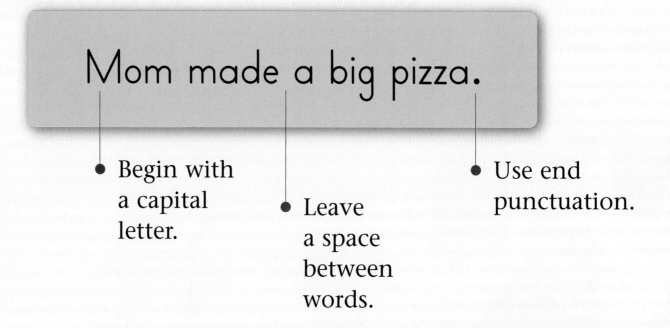

Mom made a big pizza.

- Begin with a capital letter.

- Leave a space between words.

- Use end punctuation.

# Kinds of Sentences

A **telling sentence** ends with a period.

> Sam ate the pizza.

An **asking sentence** ends with a question mark.

> Who is Sam?

An **exciting sentence** ends with an exclamation point.

> Sam is my crazy cat!

# Using Capital Letters

You use **capital letters** in your writing.

The **first word** in a sentence

> **B**ears catch fish.

**Special names**

> **S**andy   **O**hio   **S**unday

The word **I**

> When can **I** go fishing?

# Making Plurals

**Plural** means "more than one."

Add **s** for most plurals.

> friend — friend**s**

Add **es** after words ending in *s*, *x*, *ch*, and *sh*.

> glass — glass**es**     lunch — lunch**es**
> box — box**es**     dish — dish**es**

**Change the word** for a few plurals.

> child — **children**   mouse — **mice**

# Using Punctuation

Use **punctuation marks** to make your writing easier to read.

**Periods** go after telling sentences.

> Tessa likes hats.

**Periods** go between dollar and cents.

> The tall hat costs $16.00.

**Periods** go after an abbreviation.

> Mr. Cook sells hats.

**Question marks** go after asking sentences.

Who is Tessa**?**

Why is she laughing**?**

**Exclamation points** show strong feeling.

That hat is funny**!**

Wow, it's tall**!**

**Commas** keep words and numbers from running together.

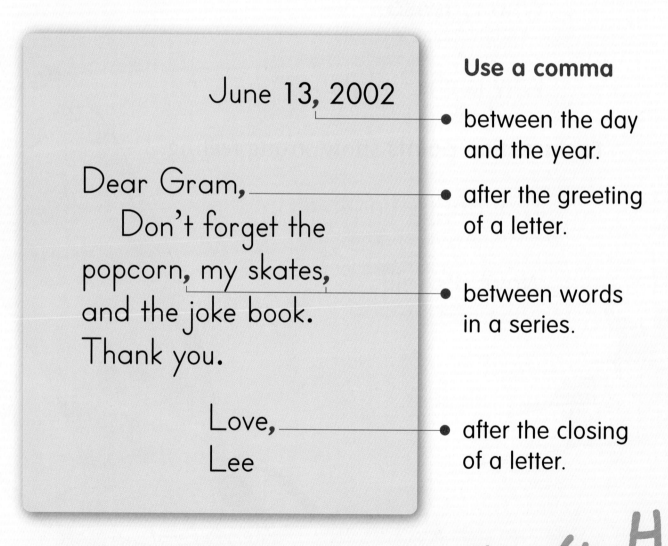

June 13, 2002

**Use a comma**

- between the day and the year.

Dear Gram,
    Don't forget the popcorn, my skates, and the joke book.
Thank you.

- after the greeting of a letter.

- between words in a series.

      Love,
      Lee

- after the closing of a letter.

**Apostrophes** show ownership.

Gram likes Lee's jokes.

**Apostrophes** make contractions.

Gram can't stop laughing.

**Quotation marks** go around a speaker's words.

Lee said, "Thanks for the joke book."
"You're welcome," said Gram.

# Understanding Our Language

The words we use are called the **parts of speech**.

A **noun** names a person, place, or thing.

> friend    park    apple

A **proper noun** names a special person, place, or thing and begins with a capital letter.

> Dave    Grant Park    McIntosh

A **pronoun** takes the place of a noun.

| | | | | |
|---|---|---|---|---|
| I | you | he | she | it |
| me | we | they | them | us |

A **verb** shows action or helps to complete a thought.

We **picked** lots of apples.
The tree **was** full of red apples.

An **adjective** describes a noun or pronoun.

Dad picked the **ripe** apples.
I ate the **biggest** one.

# Using Everyday Words

**Everyday words** are words you read and write many times a day.

**A**
about
after
again
all
always
am
and
any
are
ask
away

**B**
baby
be
because
been
before
big
book
boy
brother
but
by

**C**
called
can
car
children
come
could

**D** did
down

**E** each
eat
every

**F** family
father
find
first
for
found
friend
from
funny
**G** get
girl
give
go
going
good

**H** had
happy
has
have
he
help
her
here
him
his
house
how
**I** if
into
is

**J** jump
just
**K** keep
knew
know
**L** land
last
left
let
like
little
live
long
look
love

A
B
C
D
E
F
G
H
I
J
K
L
M
N
O
P
Q
R
S
T
U
V
W
X
Y
Z

**M**
made
make
man
many
me
more
mother
must
my

**N**
name
need
new
next
night
not
now

**O**
of
off
old
once
only
or
other
our
out
over

**P**
part
people
place
play
please
put

**Q**
question

**R**
ride
right
room
run

**S**
said
saw
say
school
she
sister
some
something
sometimes
soon
stop

**T**
take
talk
thank
that
the
their
them
then
there
they
thing
this
time
to
told
took

**U**
under
until
up
upon
us
use

**V**
very

**W**
walk
want
was
way
we
well
went
were
what

when
where
which
who
why
will
with
woman
won't
work
would
write

**Y**
yes
you
your

**Z**
zoo

# Using the Right Word

Words that sound the same but have different meanings are called **homophones**.

**ant, aunt**

> A little **ant** tickled my toe.
> My **aunt** likes to dance.

**ate, eight**

> The rabbits **ate** the carrots.
> I saw **eight** rabbits in the garden.

**blew, blue**

> The wind **blew** my hair.
> The sky is **blue** on a sunny day.

**for, four**

> I made a card **for** Mom.
> Dad ate **four** pancakes.

**hear, here**

> I **hear** Ben's cat meowing outside.
> My cat is **here** beside me.

A B C D E F G H I J K L M N O P Q R S T U V W X Y Z

A B C D E F G H I J K L M N O P Q R S T U V W X Y Z

### knew, new

> Jack **knew** Jill.
> Jill has a **new** pail.

### know, no

> Do you **know** my name?
> "**No**, I don't," said Theo.

### meat, meet

> The **meat** is on the grill.
> We'll **meet** you at the park.

**read, red**

> Kim **read** a poetry book.
> The book has a **red** cover.

**road, rode**

> Emma lives on that **road**.
> She **rode** her bike home.

**son, sun**

> Mr. Kitt's **son** lives in Florida.
> The **sun** shines a lot in Florida.

**sum, some**

> The **sum** of 2 + 2 is 4.
> Do you want **some** grapes?

**tail, tale**

> A beaver has a flat **tail**.
> Sometimes a story is called a **tale**.

**to, two, too**

> Let's go **to** the movies.
> I'll buy **two** tickets.
> Can we have popcorn, **too**?

**won, one**

> Brady **won** a gold medal.
> He has a silver **one** already.

**wood, would**

> One pig had a house of **wood**.
> Bub **would** like an ice-cream cone.

**wear, where**

> May I **wear** my new shoes?
> **Where** are my old shoes?

# Student
# Almanac

# Lists, Maps, and Theme Words

You'll love using these pages. They have helpful information, pictures, and word lists that you can use and enjoy.

B A
C
D E
F G
H
I
J
K L
M N
O
P
Q
S R
T U
V
W
X Y
Z

# Practicing Handwriting

Neat handwriting helps you and others to read and enjoy your writing.

## Handwriting Tips

- **LOOK** at handwriting models.
- **PRACTICE** letters often.
- **LEAVE** spaces between words.
- **SLANT** all letters the same way.

Write this way, or
write this way.
You'll have fun
with _Write One_!

# Manuscript Models

A B C D E F G
H I J K L M
N O P Q R S
T U V W X Y Z

a b c d e f g

h i j k l m

n o p q r s

t u v w x y z

## Continuous Stroke Models

A B C D E F G

H I J K L M

N O P Q R S

T U V W X Y Z

a b c d e f g

h i j k l m

n o p q r s

t u v w x y z

A
B C
D E
G H
I
J
K L
M N
O
P
Q
S R
T
U
V
W
X Y
Z

# Using a Computer

The more you know about a computer, the more you can do with it. You can use a computer for writing stories, sending e-mail, and many other things.

## Parts of a Computer

**Computer**
**Disk**
**Keyboard**
**Monitor**
**Mouse**
**Printer**

The mouse moves the cursor.

# Using Maps

Maps help you find places near and far.

## Map Signs

A **compass rose** shows directions. N is for North, E is for East, S is for South, and W is for West.

A **key** explains the symbols on a map.

**United States**

⭐ National Capital

–·–·–·– State Boundaries

Arctic Ocean

Arctic Ocean

**North America**

Atlantic Ocean

**Europe**

**Asia**

Pacific Ocean

**Africa**

Equator

**South America**

Indian Ocean

Pacific Ocean

**Australia**

N
W · E
S

# The World
### Continents and Oceans

**Antarctica**

B A
C
D E
G H
I
J
K
M N
O P
Q S R
T U V
W
X
Y
Z

Arctic
Ocean

Alaska
(U.S.)

**Greenland**

N
W E
S

**Canada**

**United States**

Pacific
Ocean

Atlantic
Ocean

**Mexico**

Gulf of
Mexico

**West Indies**

# North America

**Central
America**

South America

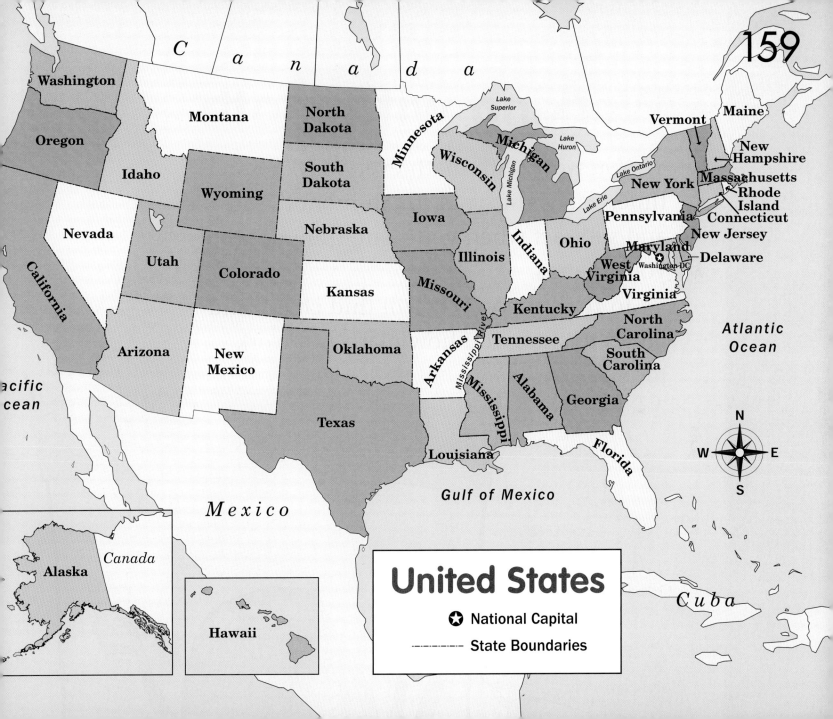

# United States

⭐ National Capital

---·--- State Boundaries

B A
C
D E
G H
I
J
K L
M N
O P
Q
S R
T U V
W
X Y
Z

# Working with Math

You work with math every day. You tell
time. You count your lunch money. You add
and subtract when you share things with
your friends.

In this section you will find charts and
tables to show you how math can work
for you.

# Telling Time

Face clocks show time with hands pointing to numbers. **Digital clocks** show time with numbers. Both of these clocks show 2:30.

hour hand

minute hand

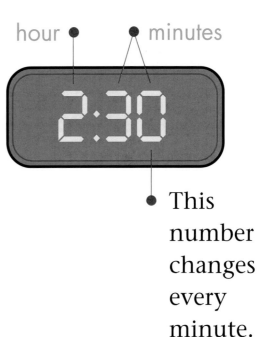

hour • • minutes

• This number changes every minute.

- The numbers on a clock face are used to tell hours and minutes.

# Numbers 1 to 100

The chart below will help you count by 1's, 5's, and 10's.

## Hundred Chart

| 1  | 2  | 3  | 4  | 5  | 6  | 7  | 8  | 9  | 10  |
|----|----|----|----|----|----|----|----|----|-----|
| 11 | 12 | 13 | 14 | 15 | 16 | 17 | 18 | 19 | 20  |
| 21 | 22 | 23 | 24 | 25 | 26 | 27 | 28 | 29 | 30  |
| 31 | 32 | 33 | 34 | 35 | 36 | 37 | 38 | 39 | 40  |
| 41 | 42 | 43 | 44 | 45 | 46 | 47 | 48 | 49 | 50  |
| 51 | 52 | 53 | 54 | 55 | 56 | 57 | 58 | 59 | 60  |
| 61 | 62 | 63 | 64 | 65 | 66 | 67 | 68 | 69 | 70  |
| 71 | 72 | 73 | 74 | 75 | 76 | 77 | 78 | 79 | 80  |
| 81 | 82 | 83 | 84 | 85 | 86 | 87 | 88 | 89 | 90  |
| 91 | 92 | 93 | 94 | 95 | 96 | 97 | 98 | 99 | 100 |

# Place Value

This chart shows what each part of a number is worth.

| hundreds | tens | ones |     |     |
|----------|------|------|-----|-----|
|          |      | 7    | =   | 7   |
|          | 1    | 0    | =   | 10  |
|          | 3    | 2    | =   | 32  |
|          | 5    | 5    | =   | 55  |
| 1        | 3    | 0    | =   | 130 |

**130 = 1** hundred, **3** tens, and **0** ones

# Bar Graphs

A **bar graph** helps you show how many.

## Children's Favorite Season

spring = 5
summer = 9
fall = 4
winter = 7

# Money

 =

one dollar = four quarters

 =

one quarter = two dimes + one nickel

 =

one dime = two nickels

 =

one nickel = five pennies

A B C D F G H I J K L M N O P Q R S T U V W X Y Z

# Addition and Subtraction

**Addition** means putting numbers together.

●●●● ●●

$$4 + 2 = 6$$

sum

- This says four plus two equals six.

**Subtraction** means taking numbers away.

✕✕✕✕●●

$$6 - 4 = 2$$

difference

- This says six minus four equals two.

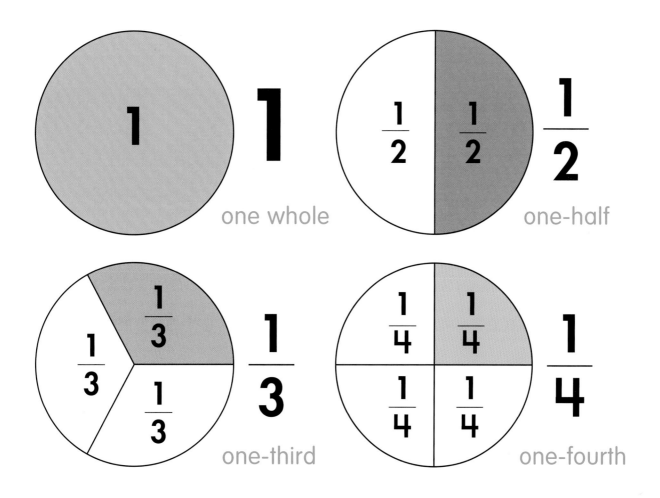

# Fractions

A **fraction** is a part of something whole.

1   one whole

$\frac{1}{2}$   $\frac{1}{2}$   one-half

$\frac{1}{3}$   one-third

$\frac{1}{4}$   one-fourth

# Using Theme Words

This chapter includes word lists for important themes you will study in school.

## Themes

- Days of the Week
- Months of the Year
- Seasons and Weather
- Numbers and Colors
- Places
- Parks
- Plants
- Food Pyramid
- Animals of the . . .
- Five Senses

# Days of the Week

Every day brings something new.

Sunday

Monday

Tuesday

Wednesday

Thursday

Friday

Saturday

# Months of the Year

There are 12 months in the year. Find your birthday month.

January

February

March

July

August

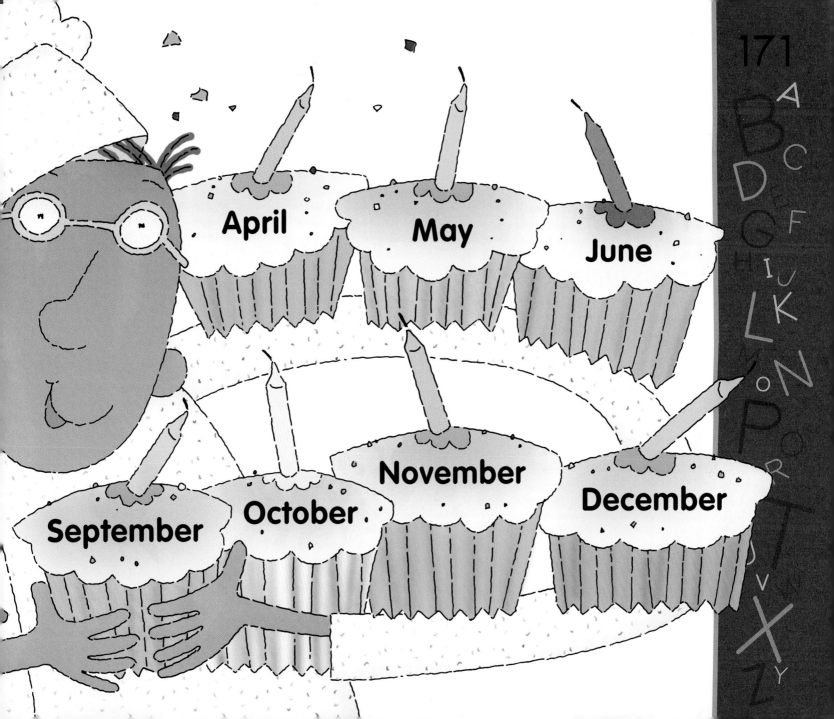

B A
C D
E
F G H
I
J
K L
M N
O
P
Q
R S
T U
V
W
X Y
Z

# Seasons and Weather

There are four seasons in a year. Each season has a different kind of weather. You use special words when you talk and write about the seasons and the weather.

## Seasons

spring

summer

# Weather Words

hot

rainy

partly sunny

sunny

lightning

cloudy

snowy

KABOOM
thunder

windy

cold

fall

winter

B A
C
D E
F G H
I
J K L
M N
O P
Q R
S
T U V
W
X Y
Z

# Numbers and Colors

Numbers and colors are everywhere!

four

three

4

two

3

blue

one

2

green

yellow

zero

1

orange

0

red

five 5

six 6

seven 7

eight 8

nine 9

ten 10

purple

pink

white

gray

brown

black

A B C D E F G H I J K L M N O

# Places

Going places is fun!

canyon

mesa

beach

desert

mountains

hills

river

forest

valley

path

# Parks

Parks are full of action.

run

swing

slide

ride

fly

camp

read

cook

# Plants

Many kinds of plants grow on earth. Garden flowers and leafy trees are two kinds of plants. These plants need sunlight, water, air, and soil to grow. Plants make oxygen that we all breathe.

Leaves use the sunlight to make food for plants.

Roots take in water and food from the soil.

grass

leaves

branches

flower

stem

trunk

roots

soil

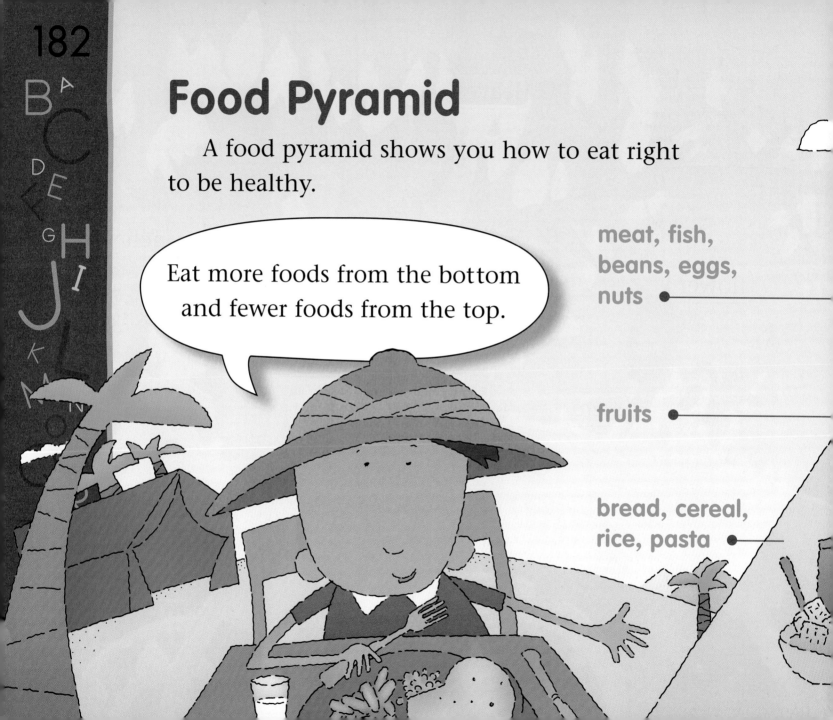

# Food Pyramid

A food pyramid shows you how to eat right to be healthy.

Eat more foods from the bottom and fewer foods from the top.

meat, fish, beans, eggs, nuts

fruits

bread, cereal, rice, pasta

fats, oils, sweets

milk, yogurt, cheese

vegetables

CHIPS

MILK

YOGURT

# Animals of the . . .

| Oceans | Woodlands | Grasslands |
| --- | --- | --- |
| crab | bear | antelope |
| fish | beaver | elephant |
| octopus | chipmunk | giraffe |
| shark | deer | hippopotamus |
| starfish | porcupine | lion |
| stingray | raccoon | prairie dog |
| whale | skunk | zebra |
| | squirrel | |

## Deserts

bat
coyote
lizard
scorpion
snake
spider

## Tropical Forests

ant
anteater
frog
monkey
parrot
sloth
tarantula

## Polar Regions

hare
penguin
polar bear
reindeer
seal
walrus

# Five Senses

I discover the world with my senses.

I **hear** with my ears,
I **taste** with my tongue,
I **see** with my eyes
  by the light of the sun.
I **touch** with my hands,
  along with my toes,
And whatever I **smell**
  tickles my nose.

# Index

The **index** can help you find information in your handbook. Let's say you want to write a letter. You can look in your index under "letters" for help.

## A

**Abbreviations**, punctuating, 130
**Addition**, 166
**Address**, envelope, 39
**Adjectives**, 135

**Alphabet**,
    Books, 52-53
    Everyday words, 136-139
    Letters, sounds, and
       words, 98-123
    Lists, 96-123
    Poem, 96-97
    Words 98-123

**Animal** words, 184-185
**Apostrophes**, 133
**Asking** sentence, 127, 131

## B

**Bar** graphs, 164
**Beginning**, writing the, 22, 67
**Blends** (consonant), 88
**Body**, of letter, 38
**Books**,
    Making your own, 52-53
    Writing about, 54-55

## C

**Calendar** words, 169-171
**Capital** letters, 126, 128
**Captions**, writing, 50-51
**Checking** writing, 26, 60, 126-145
**Cinquain** poetry, 70
**Clusters**, planning with, 40, 58
**Color** words, 174-175
**Commas**, 132
**Compound** words, 95
**Computers**, 154-155
**Consonant** sounds, 98-123
    Blends, 88
    Digraphs, 89
**Context** of a word, 84-85, 87
**Continuous** stroke
      handwriting, 152-153
**Contractions**, 94, 133
**Couplet**, 68

## D

**Dates**, punctuation of, 132
**Days** of the week, 169
**Declarative** sentence, 127, 130
**Description**, writing, 46-47
**Dialogue**, 133
**Digraphs** (consonant), 89
**Directions**, writing, 48-49
**Dramatic** reading, 55
**Drawing**, planning with, 24, 30, 66

## E

**E-mail** messages, 36-37
**Ending**, writing the, 22, 67
**Everyday** words, 136-139
**Exciting** sentence, 127, 131
**Exclamation** points, 127, 131
**Exclamatory** sentence, 127, 131

## F

**First** draft, 25, 59
**Five** senses, 186-187
**Food** pyramid, 182-183
**Friendly** letters, 38-39
**Friendly** notes, 34-35

## G

**Graphs**, 162-164
**Group** work, 80-81

## H

**Handwriting**, 148-153
**Homophones**, 140-145
**How-to** writing, 48-49
**Hundred** chart, 162

## I

**Ideas** for writing, 12-21, 31, 33, 35, 45, 49, 63, 73
**Interrogative** sentence, 127, 131
**Invitation**, 34

## J

**"Jenny Writes,"** 12-21
**Journal** writing, 30-31

## L

**Learning** logs, 62-63

**Letters**, friendly, 38
    Addressing the envelope, 39
    E-mail, 36-37
    Friendly notes, 34-35
    Punctuating, 132

**List** poem, 71
**Listening** skills, 76-77
**Lists**, planning with, 24, 52
**Lists**, writing, 32-33

## M

**Manuscript** handwriting, 150-151
**Maps**, using, 156
  North America, 158
  United States, 159
  The world, 157
**Math** skills,
  Addition, 166
  Bar graphs, 164
  Fractions, 167
  Money, 165
  Numbers 1 to 100, 162
  Place-value chart, 163
  Subtraction, 166
  Telling time, 161
**Mechanics** of writing, 128-133
**Middle**, writing the, 22, 67
**Money**,
  Counting, 165
  Punctuating amounts of, 130
**Months** of the year, 170-171

## N

**Notes**, friendly, 34-35
**Nouns**, 134
**Number** words, 174-175
**Numbers** 1 to 100, 162

## O

**Ocean** names, 157

**Organizing** ideas,
  Clusters, 40, 58
  Directions, writing, 48-49
  Lists, 24, 52
  Story plans, 40, 66

## P

**Park** words, 178-179
**Parts** of speech, 134-135
**Patterns**,
  Vowel, 90-91
  Writing, 72-73
**Periods**, 130
**Phonics**, using, 88-123
  Sounding out words, 86-87
**Place-value** chart, 163
**Place** words, 176-177
**Planning** writing, 24, 40, 52, 58, 66
**Plant** words, 180-181
**Plural** words, 129
**Poems**, writing, 68-71
  About books, 54
**Possessives**, 133
**Poster**, making a, 55
**Prewriting**, 24, 40, 52, 58, 66
**Pronouns**, 135

**Proofreading,** 26, 60, 126-145
**Proper** nouns, 134
**Publishing,** 27, 53, 61
**Punctuation** marks, 126-127, 130-133
**Pyramid,** food, 182-183

## Q

**Quatrain,** 69
**Question** marks, 127, 131
**Questions,** 127, 131
**Quotation** marks, 133

## R

**Reading,**
    Everyday words, 136-139
    New words, 86-87
    Theme words, 168-187
    Understanding, 84-85
    Using the alphabet, 98-123
    Your writing, 26-27, 60-61

**Reports,** 58-61
**Retelling,** book, 55
**Reviews,** book, 54-55
**Revising** writing, 26, 60
**Rhyming,**
    Families, 92-93
    Pattern writing, 72-73
    Poems, 68-69

**Right** word, using, 140-145
**Rules** for writing, 126-145

## S

**Seasons** and weather words, 172-173
**Senses** words, 186-187
    Using in writing, 46-47
**Sentences,** writing, 126
    Kinds of, 127
**Sharing** writing, 14-18, 27, 53, 61
**Show-and-tell** tips, 79
**Sounding** out words, 86-87
**Speaking** skills, 78-79

**Spelling,**
    Alphabet words, 98-123
    Everyday words, 136-139
    Phonetic patterns, 90-93
    Theme words, 168-187

**Stories,** writing, 66-67
    About me, 40-41
    About others, 44-45

## T

**Telling** sentences, 127
**Thank-you** note, 35
**Theme** words, 168-187
**Tongue** twister, 70
**Traits** of good writing, 22-23

## U

**Understanding** our language, 134-135
**Using** the right word, 140-145

## V

**Verbs**, 135
**Vocabulary**,
    Context of a word, 87
    Everyday words, 136-139
    Homophones, 140-145
    Reading new words, 86-87
**Vowel** sounds, 90, 91, 98,
        102, 106, 112, 118, 122
    Long and short, 90-91

## W

**Weather** words, 173

**Words**, reading and writing,
    Alphabet, 98-123
    Compound, 95
    Contractions, 94
    Everyday, 136-139
    Homophones, 140-145
    Long vowels, 90
    Rhyming, 92-93
    Short vowels, 91
    Theme, 168-187

**Writing**,
    About books, 54-55
    About experiences, 30-31, 40-41
    About facts, 52-53, 58-61, 62-63
    Captions, 50-51
    Descriptions, 46-47
    Directions, 48-49
    E-mail messages, 36-37
    How-to, 48-49
    Journals, 30-31
    Learning logs, 62-63
    Letters, 38-39
    Lists, 32-33
    Notes, 34-35
    Patterns, 72-73
    Poetry, 68-71
    Reports, 58-61
    Sentences, 126-127
    Stories, 40-41, 44-45, 66-67
    Traits of good, 22-23

**Writing** process, 12-21
    Checking, 26, 60, 126-145
    First draft, 25, 59
    Planning, 24, 40, 52, 58, 66
    Publishing, 27, 53, 61
    Revising, 26, 60
    Steps in, 24-27